POODLE COLLECTIBLES

of the 50's & 60's

by
Elaine Butler

photographed by
Brenda Bohannon

* Most of the photography was done by Brenda Bohannon.
A small amount of pictures were taken by other collectors.

Published by

L-W BOOK SALES
P.O. Box 69
Gas City, IN 46933

ISBN#: 0-89538-038-2

Published by: L-W BOOK SALES
P.O. Box 69
Gas City, IN 46933

Printed by IMAGE GRAPHICS, INC., Paducah, Kentucky

Please write for our free catalog.

Attention Collectors . . . if you would like to contribute photographs or information of your collection (possibly for profit), please call L-W Books (toll free) at 1-800-777-6450 Tuesday thru Friday 9am to 3pm EST.

Table of Contents

Acknowledgments

The behind the scenes story of this (and probably most) book may be as interesting as the book itself. With that said I won't elaborate.

I want to say a special thanks to my parents, my mom who bought the tiny brooch years ago, and my dad from whom I inherited the love of writing. I also want to thank my husband and children. I'm sure they have nightmares that pink poodles are taking over the planet. Thanks to Dan VanArsdale for loaning many of the jewelry items for photos and to Debbie LiBrandi for the notes of encouragement. Finally a very special thanks to Betty Pruett who opened her home to Brenda and me to photograph a portion of her collection and for opening her heart in friendship.

Preface

One of many fond memories from my childhood is a day I spent shopping with my mother. On that particular day I came away with an inexpensive rhinestone poodle brooch. I remember admiring the tiny treasure all the way home and wearing it often. Eventually, however, the pin was lost but never completely forgotten.

Years later as an adult I saw a similar poodle pin at a flea market. I bought it, and began searching for an exact duplicate to the brooch I had as a child. I never found the exact duplicate, but did find many other irresistible poodle pins. Soon my interest broadened. I began to notice other poodle trinkets and I joined the throng of adult baby boomers attempting to buy back their childhood.

During my search for these whimsies I discovered there were other collectors of poodle paraphernalia. I also discovered an almost unbelievable diversity in the poodle kitsch still available. When I began searching for more information on what was available I found very little had been written, and the idea for this book was born.

As with most collectors, I sometimes become overzealous in my search for the collection. The intent for the book is, however, a sportive tone. It would somehow seem unfair to these mirthful creatures to burden them with anything too serious.

Pricing

It's been said that it takes a thick-skinned individual to write a price guide. The prices in this book are retail and are intended to be taken generally. Damaged pieces unless they are extremely rare have little value to most collectors: therefore all prices listed are for mint condition items. There has been some flexibility in standards, for example an unused paper item may be priced as "mint" even though it has yellowed with age, or an older linen item may be somewhat fragile due to natural process.

The prices are based on my observations. Some items will be higher because they crossover into more than one field of collectibles. It goes without saying that geography will always play a role in the pricing of any collectible.

I have tried very hard to be fair to both dealer and collector in the price guide listed.

Introduction

Mention the fabulous fifties and what comes to mind? Roy Rogers, Elvis, beatniks and saddle shoes are forever affiliated with that decade. Ponytails, T.V. Dinners and 45 Records go hand in hand with the childhood of the baby boom generation. There is nothing however, more synonymous with the fifties than the "French Poodle". For over a decade these capricious creatures adorned everything from the top of the new television to the napkin at the cocktail lounge. Poodles could be found peeking from the ladies skirt tails and hanging on the bathroom towel racks.

Following World War II the poodle and Parisienne strutted straight into the heart of American culture. It's been speculated that the popularity of all things French during America's mid century was a result of the returning servicemen's experience in France.

Ironically the poodle may not have originated in France at all. There seems to be no doubt that the poodle originated in Europe. Which European country first bred the poodle is highly debated. Some sources say France, some say Germany and others say Russia. The word poodle came from the German word pudein (to splash water). The dogs were originally called Pudelhunds, which was later shortened to pudel. It is hard to imagine Fi Fi and Pierre as Otto and Matilda. Even more difficult to comprehend would be the dog's origination in Russia. Imagine the epitome of American fifties culture being Russian. Good ole Joe McCarthy is probably spinning in the grave at the mere suggestion.

It is widely accepted that poodles were originally used by hunters as water retrievers. The flamboyant coiffures worn by the breed were first implemented to make it easier for the dog to swim. The pom poms at the joints were believed to protect from rheumatism. Even the ribbons in the hair had a purpose, they were used by the hunters in various colors to identify their dogs. The French may have been the first to use the poodles in the circus and thus the French poodle was born.

Whatever it's genesis, no other breed could have been more suited to the mid century modernism. The most decorative of dogs for the most extremely decorative of decades. In the post war America the poodle went from the twenty-fifth most popular breed in 1946 to surpass the beagle for the number one spot in 1960. The poodle reigned as the most often registered breed until 1983 when the cocker spaniel took the throne as the most registered.

To be labeled French in mid century U.S. was the essence of high fashion and of course poodles were "French". No self respecting starlet would be found poodleless, or at the very least she would have one available for photo sessions. The most sophisticated of ladies would dye their poodles to match their outfits.

Poodles seemed to show up in some form in all areas of life in the American fifties. To borrow a threadbare but irreplaceable phrase there were "Oodles of Poodles". So relax, turn the page and explore culture a'la poodle.

CHAPTER 1

Kitchen Canines

Ceramic Container with lid,
copyright 1962. Marked
on lid Besshunferl,
by Goebel Germany.
$25-30

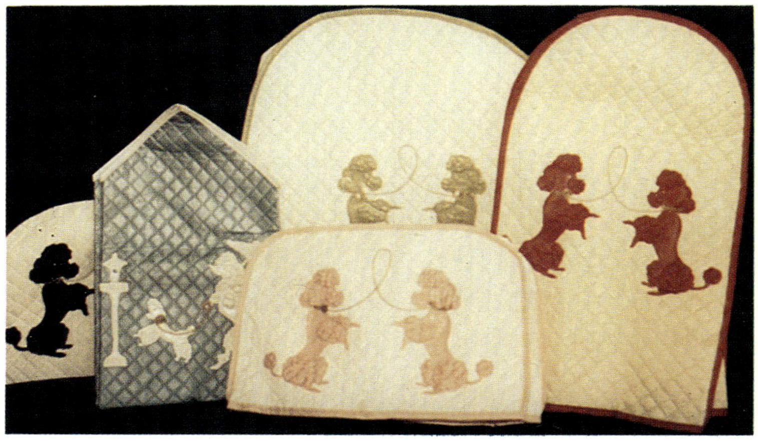

Appliance Covers in various shapes, sizes, designs and colors.
$8-10 each

Egg shaped Platter,
marked "Holland".
$15-20

Fanciful Poodles embellish cannister set
by Ransburg of Indianapolis.
$35-45

Almond Kisses chocolate tin,
marked Barton's bonbonniere.
$3-6

Poodle Serving Tray
marked "Made in Calif. U.S.A".
$10-15

Poodle Toast Carts,
marked "Japan".
$15-20

Casserole is "Chi Chi" poodle.
pattern, marked "Glidden 167".
$30-40

This black satin Apron was
most likely worn by a waitress or bar maid.
$10-15

This Apron is from a Cut & Sew kit.
$4-6

Bib Apron,
from a Cut & Sew kit.
$4-6

This Apron was pre-stamped
for embroidery.
$4-6

Factory made Apron, no label.
$8-10

An Apron from a preprinted kit.
$4-6

Poodle Cookie Jar, unmarked.
$30-40

Cookie Counter Cookie Jar, by Twin Winton.
$75-100

Cookie Jar by Sierra Vista Ceramics, Pasadena, Calif.
$75-100

On the left is a planter that is marked "Reliable Glassware and Pottery 1956". The cookie jar at the right is unmarked. The planter appears to go with the cookie jar.

Planter – $15-20
Cookie Jar – $30-40

Poodle sitting on a stool, unmarked cookie jar.
$30-40

Three clear glasses from a set of six, with black poodles, trimmed with a gold design around the top.
$15-20

Elegant frosted glasses in a rack. Gold and black poodles with rhinestone collars decorate these glasses, signed Maida Armour.

$50-60 per set with rack

Set of four Juice Glasses.

$10-15 per set

This tall slim glass was also made in at least one other size.

$4-6 each

Small Plastic Tumbler (possibly hand painted).

$3-4 each

Frosted glass with Fi Fi La Poodle pictured on it.

$3-6 each

Small Glass with a show cut poodle standing among the stars.
$4-5 each

This is a set of 6 glass tumblers, the dogs on this set have a fuzzy texture. The glass swizzle sticks came separately.
$20-25 a set

Fi Fi and Pepe Tumblers, set of 8 glasses with original box, (mint condition).
$30-40 a set

Cocktail Napkins two different types of poodles shown.
$4-7 each

Cocktail Napkins with paper labels marked "Handmade by Leacock in Madera".
$15-18 a pair

Cocktail Napkins – **$4-6**

Cotton fabric panels for a clip and sew skirt. The edge of the fabric has printed instructions.
$30-40

Cocktail Napkin
$6-8

Terrycloth Christmas Pot Holder
$4-6

Tablecloth with poodle playing ball, no label.
$25-30

Tablecloth picturing poodles with a bone, no label.
$25-30

Fitted Bridge Tablecloth, no label. **$15-20**

Terry Dish Towl, no label. **$4-6**

Polka Dot Tablecloth with a canine border, no label.
$20-25

Linen Towl, marked Let's Go to Paris!
$6-8

Terrycloth Kitchen Towel, with a turquoise pedigree and a pink mongrel, marked on towel "What's Cooking? Quick Dry". Paper label marked "Parisian Prints".
$8-10

Dish Towel with a
poodle in an apron, no label.
$4-6

Colorful Linen Dish Towel with blue poodle.
$4-6

Poodle puppy with a
ball and bone on a
Linen Dish Towel.
$4-6

Linen Dish Towel with a poodle cook,
in a faddish chartreuse and gold color.
$6-8

Two Linen Tea Towels, hand embroidered.
The one marked Dolls on the right most likely had a male mate.
$5-7 each

Two Linen Tea Towels, nicely embroidered.
$12-16 a pair

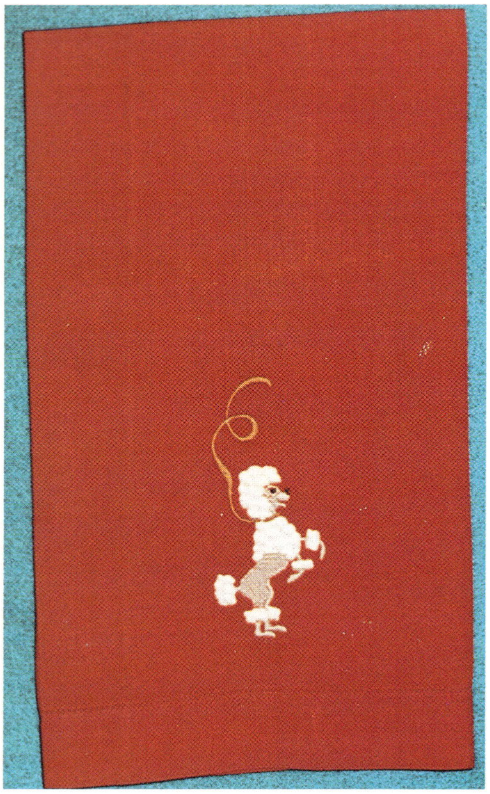

Linen Tea Towel, no label.
$4-6

One of the several colors of the Park Avenue Tea Towels.
$6-8

Tea Towel, unlabeled.
$4-6

Machine embroidered Linen Tea Towel.
$4-6

Tea Towel, machine embroidered, with leashed poodle.
$4-6

Saucer with a paper label marked "Josef Originals".
$7-10

These poodle plates have a paper label marked "Chase Made in Japan".
Hedi Schoop made an almost identical pair.
These are possibly an unauthorized spin-off of them.
$20-25 a pair

A Metal Plate with a performing poodle.
This plate is signed Geo Briard.
$10-15

Enameled Metal Plate with paper label marked "Handcrafted of Cheshire Conn."
$12-16

"Chi Chi" Poodle Dinnerware by Glidden. These saucers also came in an identical pattern without the borders. This saucer has an in mold mark "Glidden 35".
$20-25

This poodle saucer by Glidden has an in mold mark "Glidden 35". This is the same marking as found on the other saucer with different patterns by Glidden.
$20-25

Kitchen Canines

(Salty Dogs)

These Salt and Peppers are currently in production by Vandor.
(They are so reminiscent of the fifties, I couldn't resist including them.)
$16-20

The black and white pair on the left are marked "Japan".
$10-12

The nicely detailed Couple on the right are by "Lefton".
$15-20

Two different pairs of Salt and Peppers,
the two on the left have angora on them, both sets are marked "Japan".
$10-12 a pair

Even the poodle wasn't too sophisticated
to go on the fire hydrant, marked "Japan".
$12-16

Left: Snooty pair of salt and peppers marked "Japan".
$15-20

Right: Lone Lady marked "Enesco Bar Hound",
(not pictured is her mate, a greyhound).
Lone Lady $10-12

This pair of Salt and Peppers, he with his monocle and she with her lorgnette, are opera bound, marked "109".
$15-20

Hobnail Salt & Peppers, marked "E 2167".
$12-16

Salt and Peppers marked "Japan".
$8-10

Poodles in a basket Salt & Pepper Shakers.
$12-14

These delightful Salt & Peppers appear to match the poodle on the heart ashtray.

Salt & Peppers $12-14

Ashtray $8-10

This is a mismatched pair of Salt and Peppers. The one on the left is by "Ceramic Arts Studio of Madison Wisconsin". She originally came with a green pillow base.

The one on the right is a "Goebel".

$10-12 each single shaker

"Primping Poodle" is recent but now discontinued by "Clay Art".
$15-20

Left: These Salt and Peppers are "Bone China".

Right: These Salt and Peppers are "Enesco". Enesco also made a larger version of Figurines like these salt and peppers.

$12-14 a pair

Gi Gi Thermos by "Aladdin" . She flirts with her beau in front of the Eiffel Tower.
$30-35

Thermos by "Aladdin" marked Suzette, she is romping near the Eiffel Tower, lunch box is not shown.
$30-35

Gi Gi Lunch Box, (this matches the thermos above)
$225-275

Figural metal Soda Bottle Opener.
$10-15

Butter Dish and Pitcher, by "Enesco".
$20-25 each

Sugar, Creamer, Ashtray, and Salt and Pepper Shakers,
all marked "Enesco".
Sugar & Creamer $20-25
Salt & Pepper $15-20
Ashtray $10-15

This set of five Trays by "Kentley, Grand Rapids, MI". Each tray features a different scene with a story of the "Romance of Fi Fi and Pepe" on the back.
$30-40

Garnier Decanter
with corkscrew.
$15-20

Pink Poodle Decanter
marked "Japan".
$15-20

Snooty Decanter with hanging glasses, unmarked.
$15-20

Poodle Decanter with Cups that
are made of red clay with black glaze, marked "Japan".
$15-20

Mama Poodle with her Pups Spice Holder.
$20-25

Snack-Sack Place Mats, red plaid material, by "Poodle Chef Creations, Milla of California".
$10-12 each

This is part of the Advertisement that went along with the above picture.

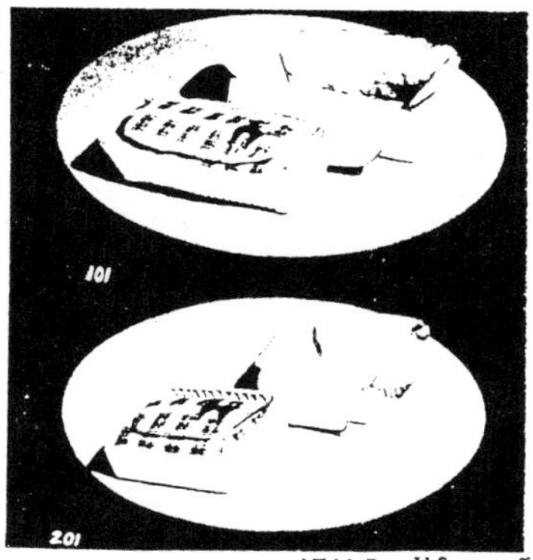

*T.M. Reg. U.S. pat. office

Poodle Chef Hostess accessories

They're sizzling-red plaid denim!
They're *Fiberglas insulated!
They're so easy to keep clean!
... just wash under faucet as you would your hands because ...
They're vinyl lined and interlined ... *Fiberglas insulation stays clean and soft as new!
They're smart ... gay ... practical!

Gourmet Cozies ... They're new! They're *Fiberglas insulated to keep hot-from-the-oven taste-appeal throughout the meal.
NO. 101. KING cozy — 19"x8"x4"
NO. 201. JUNIOR cozy — 11"x8"x2"

© Poodle Chef creations by MILLA of california

plastic factors · 414 el camino · san carlos · calif.

You have selected one of a new, distinctive group of hostess accessories. Each is a design original by MILLA of California ... developed to make modern casual party-planning easier. Once you've used MILLA accessories, you'll quickly adopt them for daily use and unusual gifts.

Nothing's too hot to hold when you're protected with Poodle Chef Mits and Holders. Vinyl lined! *Fiberglas insulated!
NO. 801. Safety-Pad Pot Holder
NO. 701. Poodle Chef Mit

Handy-Pockets Aprons ... 3 big pockets to hold mit, pot holder ... chef's gadgets.
NO. 501. HOST Handy-Pockets Apron
NO. 401. HOSTESS Handy-Pockets Apron
NO 601. POODLE CHEF Hat.

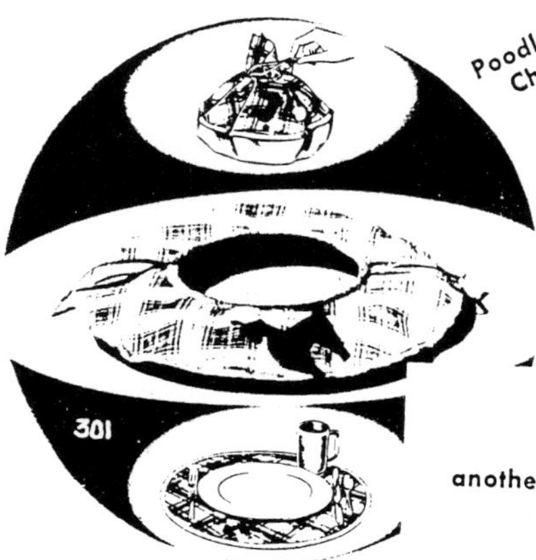

Poodle Chef SNACK-SACK place mats

Brand new! The place-mat carry-all!

Opens to hold plate, silver, cup, napkin.

Pre-pack individual, party place-settings in the Snack-Sack carry-all ... keeps them clean, dust-free and ready for use. Guests remove place-settings, spread Snack-Sack flat and it's an attractive, 18" round table mat. Sizzling-red plaid and solid-color denim. Perfect party conversation starter!
NO. 301

another original by MILLA of california

This is part of the Advertisement
that went along with the Snack-Sack Place Mats.

CHAPTER 2

Household Helpers/Poodles with a Purpose

(Poodles A'la Cart)

Poodle pulling a cart, not marked by any maker. Possibly made by Napco, the same as the other poodles pulling carts that follow.
$20-25

Poodle pulling a cart, stamped "1G2253".
$20-25

Poodle pulling a cart, with a paper label marked "Napco", stamped "1G2253".
$20-25

Napco made many versions of this cart all with different poodles. This one is unmarked.
$20-25

Poodle pulling a cart Planter, 9" x 14", very large, no label.
$30-40

Plaid and Polka Dotted Poodle pulling a cart, unmarked.
$10-12

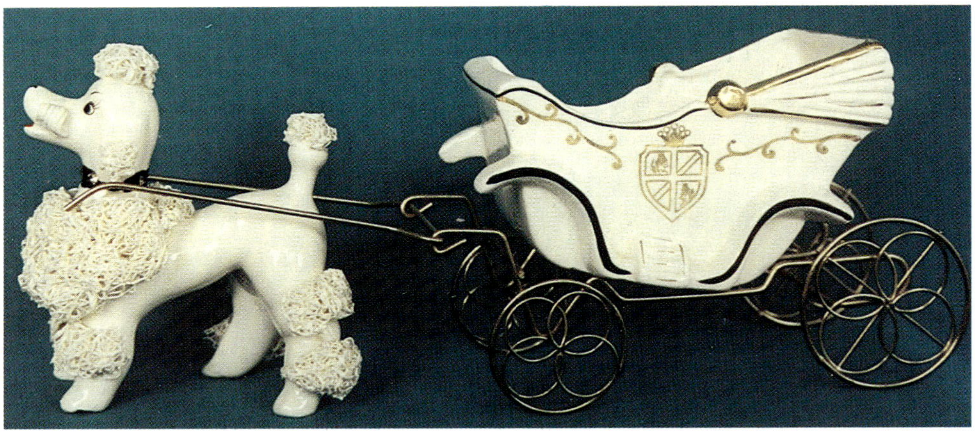

Show Cut Poodle pulls a Carriage in a wire holder.
The dog and carriage are stamped "1G2254" with a paper label marked "Napco".
$25-30

Poodle pulling a cart, unmarked.
$15-20

Household Helpers/Poodles with a Purpose

(Trashy Dogs)

Trash Can with Dutch Cut Poodle pictured, unmarked.
$20-25

Trash Can by "Ransburg", also has a matching toilet seat.
$20-25

Trash Can with lacy cut border, unmarked. (This trash can matches the hamper on page 46).
$25-30

Trash Can with Poodle on a leash, unmarked.
$20-25

Household Helpers/Poodles with a Purpose

(Poodle Time)

Poodle Wind-Up Clock
in a ceramic case, unmarked.
$20-25

Chalkware Poodle with Clock.
$30-40

Animated French Poodle Clock by California Clock Company.
This was made with and without rhinestones and in at least five colors.
$50-75

Household Helpers/Poodles with a Purpose

(Poodle Lamps)

Poodle Lamp, unmarked.
The dealer I bought it from had written Cordey on the price sticker.
$175-200

Poodle Puppy Night Light, unmarked.
$20-25

T.V. Lamp with in mold mark "Lanet & Co., L.A. Calif. 1956".
$50-60

A Pair of Night Lights,
both have indentions in the top of the hats possibly perfume lamps, no label.
$25-30 each

"Modern" Ameba shaped base lamp with a fiberglass shade, no markings.
$40-45

Wooden Child's Lamp, a white poodle.
$15-20

A Child's plaster poodle lamp, unmarked.
$20-25

A brown pottery lamp base poodle, marked "Japan".
$20-25

Poodle Lamp, unmarked, possibly Cordey.
$125-150

Household Helpers/Poodles with a Purpose

(Banking on Poodles)

Bank with Poodle tied to the Eiffel Tower, marked on lid "Penny Saver", on jar "For My Cadillac", no label.
$15-20

Poodle Bank that closes with a lock around its neck, unmarked.
$15-20

Poodle Bust Bank, no label.
$20-25

Poodle Bank with an in mold mark "Pinto L.A.". The cork stopper has a paper label that reads "Hand Painted, made in California by Pinto Products".
$20-25

Jewelry Box with double doors.
$60-80

Kleenex Holders, metal, marked "Ransbury".
$18-22 each

Ring Holder, goldtone metal poodle offers a raised tail to hold rings.
$6-8

Avon Perfume Bottles with original box.
The white poodle contains Cotillion,
and the black one contains Field Flowers.
$3-6 each

Poodle Perfume Holders,
sweet smelling pets hold your
favorite perfume, no label.
$25-40 each

Poodle Lipstick Holder,
marked "Japan".
$6-8

Two different Poodle Bubble Bath Bottles,
labels are gone.
$6-8

Powder Box (rare), and Perfume Bottle which also came in blue or white. Paper label marked "Thames". Sold as a three piece set with two perfume bottles by Sears in the mid 1950's.
$40-60 a set

Pink Shower Curtain with diverse Parisian scenes adorn this curtain.
$20-30

These homemade cozies are designed to cover the spare toilet paper and bar of soap. They are two of hundreds of versions.
$3-6 each

Toilet Paper Dispenser, with an ornate pink lady poodle.
$25-35

Chalk Poodle Lady in Bathtub with "Bathometer", marked "Miller Studios 1973." (The poodle's popularity declined, but did continue into the 1970's).
$8-12

This toilet seat is the ultimate example of 1950's kitsch.
$40-50

Fi Fi is on the right shown with the original box and her companion is on the left.
$10-15 each

Left to Right: Toothbrush Holder, Soap Dish, and a nail brush. All marked "Japan".
$10-15 each

Bath Towels by "Lila Lou",
they came in a decorative gift box.
$15-20

Hand Towels, no label.
$4-6 each

Gift Set by "Cannon".
$12-18 a set

Tray and Glasses with gold trim, may have been used for a bathroom vanity, marked "Austria".
$30-40 a set

Rare Clothes Hamper, marked "Pearl Wick, Long Island, NY", combines inseparable themes of Poodles and Parisian.
$60-75

Quilted Child's Hamper, no label.
$30-45

Clothes Hamper, patterned vinyl with lucite handle, no label.
$60-75

Household Helpers/Poodles with a Purpose

(Smoke Break)

Ashtrays, marked "Sascha Brastoff California". Sascha's ceramics are the epitome of mid century modern.
$20-25 each

Cigarette Holder and Matching Ashtrays, no label.
$30 a set

Glass Ashtray with metal frame.
$10-15

Poodle sitting on an Ashtray.
$8-12

Mama and her litter, guarding the ashtray.
$8-12

Blue and White Stuffed Poodle,
holding an aluminum ashtray,
(a sure fire hazard).
$6-8

Dreamy Eyed Poodle
adorns this ashtray.
$12-14

Poodle Ashtray, marked "Japan".
$12-14

Poodle Cigarette Lighters.
(The goldtone figural on the far left is "Florenza").
$20-40 each

Matchbox
$3-5

Left: Pink Poodle and Pups in Ashtray, marked "Lefton".

Right: Black Poodle in Ashtray,
reads "Can't understand how it happened",
marked "Made in U.S.A. California".
$10-15 each

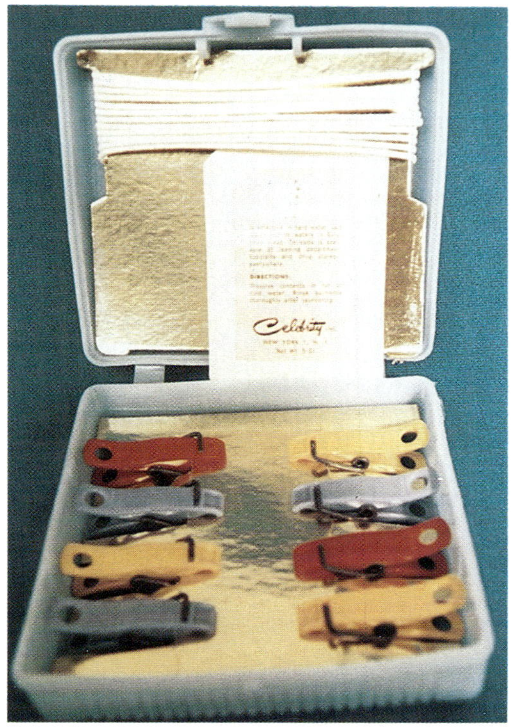

Blue plastic box holds a Traveling Clothesline and Clothespins, complete with "Cel Suds" detergent packet.
$20-22

This poodle figure used for this door knocker can also be found on a phone dialer and a pen holder.
$20-25

Grey Poodle Laundry Sprinkler, marked "Japan".
$30-35

Ceramic Poodle Handle to hold
the lint brush, "Japan".
$15-20

Elegant Poodle Candle Holders.
$30-40 pair

Pink Patio Table with a glass holder
in each corner. (Rare)
$150-200

Wire and wrought iron, magazine rack.
$125-150

Telephone Dialer, no marks.
$12-16

Ink Pen Holder, made of heavy metal, holds a pen in the coil to make the tail.
$18-22

Poodle Letter Holder with a stamp dispenser.
$18-22

Poodle Pal Letter Holder with original box has many features, a pen, ruler, letter opener, sponge for sealing letters, etc. (The sponge usually has disintegrated with age).
$20-25 with box

Poodle Bookends, marked "Japan".
$10-15 pair

Two Poodle Figurines on Bookends, marked "Japan".
$15-20 pair

Poodle Bookends made of red clay, marked "Japan".
$10-15 a pair

Bookends with Pen Holders, marked "Japan".
$10-15 a pair

White Poodle Struts on planter, "Royal Copley".
$6-8

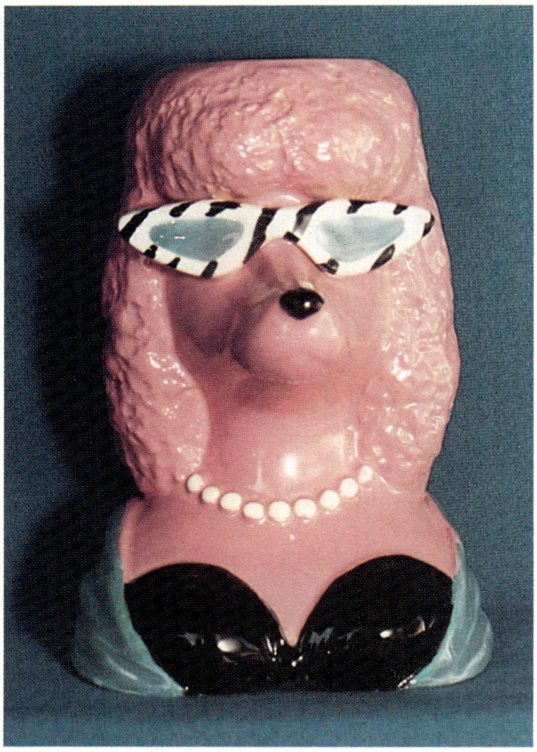

Planter which is now out of production, unmarked. Despite her very 50's style, she was actually produced by Vandor in the 1980's.
$10-15

Poodle holding white Porcelain Vase, trimmed in gold, (I suspect it's by Lefton), numbered "1632".
$20-25

Poodle Planter, by "McCoy".
$20-25

CHAPTER 3

Decor D'Arf

Poodle holding its paw up, paper label reads "Wales made in Japan".
$8-12

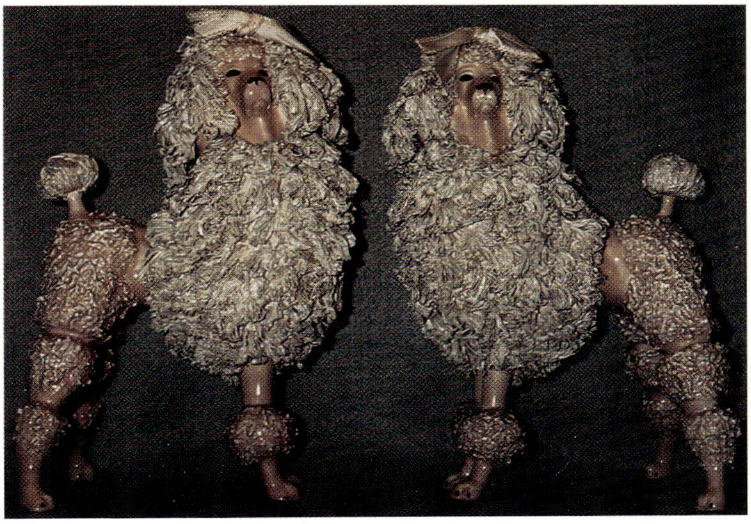

This unmarked elegant pair of Poodles stand $10^{1/2}$" tall, and would definitely be a fine focal point in any collection.
$350-400 a pair

Three Senior Poodles out for a stroll, the one on the left has a paper label marked "Chase Handpainted Japan".
$12-16 each

Estelle, by Basil Matthews.
$60-70

Mom with her Pups,
by Kreiss & Co., paper tag
around the mom's neck reads
"High Society Park Ave. Blue Blood".
$15-20

Graduate Poodle with its Proud Mother,
both are stamped "52/289". The graduate also has a
paper label that reads "Thames Handpainted Japan".
$15-20 each

Unusual Silver Poodle, unmarked.
$18-22

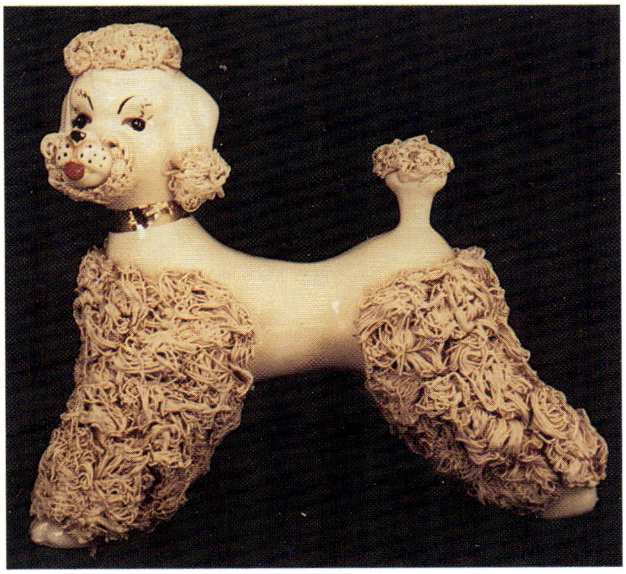

Ceramic Poodle, with gold collar.
This extra large figurine is a great example of the ceramic work often referred to as "spaghetti".
$60-65

Poodle with Studded Collar,
paper label reads "Lefton".
$15-20

Two matching poodles, unmarked.
$25-40 a pair

A rare turquoise figurine with slaw trim.
(Although turquoise was a popular color of the 1950's, there are very few turquoise poodle figurines).
$30-35

Poodle, unmarked.
$10-15

Poodle, unmarked.
$10-15

Poodle Easter Basket.
$10-15

This pair of Poodles could pass for part giraffe and zebra, paper label reads "Enesco made in Japan".
$12-16 a pair

Left: Poodle with a Bow Tie, with a paper label "Thames made in Japan". This figurine has a smaller version salt & pepper set with a cat as the mate.

Right: Poodle with the hat, unmarked.

$15-20 each

Left: Snooty Poodle Figurine with gold collar, has a paper label "Norcrest Fine China Japan", also made in a smaller size salt & pepper shaker set.

Right: Poodle with flower collar, unmarked.

$12-15 each

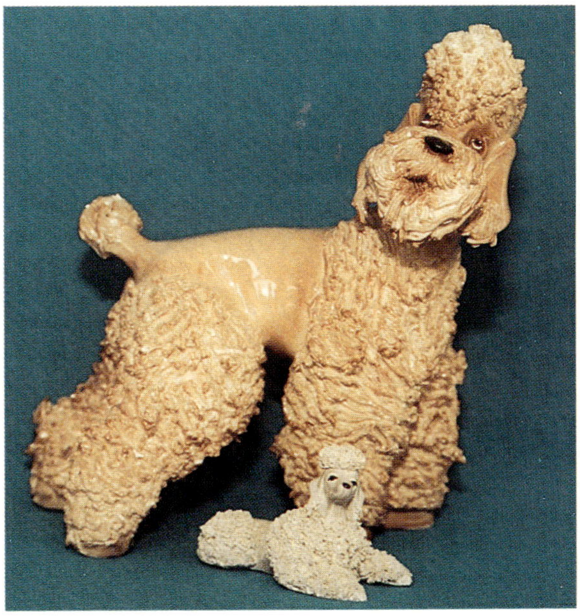

The small poodle is stamped "Hardie Arnita", the large poodle has a paper label marked "Hardie".

Small Poodle - $20-25
Large Poodle - $60-65

Poodle Huggies are stamped "E-1795", they also have a paper label that reads "Inarco Japan".

$15-20 a pair

Prissy Porcelain Pair by Lefton, came in pink and blue as well.
$45-55 a pair

This enormous ceramic poodle is 14$^{1/2}$" tall and has the faintest of marks "Calif Ceramics".
$70-75

Dancing Poodles (The Last Tango in Paris).
$20-25

Pink Lady Poodle with blue rhinestone eyes, accented with "cole slaw" look, with gold collar.
$60-75

Pink Poodle Lady by Lefton,
has a swollen nose due to a bee sting.
Marked "KB80552 Lefton China Hand
Painted".
$20-25

Delicate porcelain poodle figurine
by Lefton has an unpictured mate
standing on all fours.
$15-20

Black angora adorns this
white ceramic poodle.
$8-12

White angora on a white ceramic poodle,
marking is illegible.
$12-16

Yvonne by Hagen Renaker,
the paper label is on her back.
$35-40

Poodle is a Royal Doulton Figurine, marked "#HN2631
and was in production from 1952-1985.
$140-160

Primitive style poodle has a yellow
tag attached to the ear marked
"Certificato origine made in Italy".
$50-60

Black and white Poodle Figurines,
unmarked glass pair.
$15-20 a pair

These two beautiful figurines are by Hutschenreuther of Bavaria.
$100-150 each

Stylized pottery poodle, unmarked.
$40-50

The large standing Poodle figurine is marked "Italy".
$40-50

The two smaller poodles are marked "Lefton". Lefton also made a begging version with the shell theme.
$30-35 each

Red clay poodles.
$5-10 each

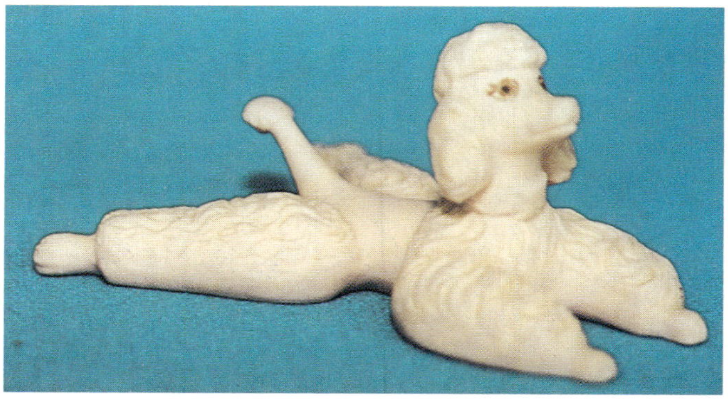

Poodle lying down, unmarked.
$8-10

Poodle with basket in her mouth,
a Staffordshire spin-off, marked "Italy".
$20-25

Tiny blown glass poodle, unmarked.
$8-10

Decor D'Arf

(Spectacled Pets)

Two poodles wearing glasses, unmarked.
$20-25 each

Left: Dog sitting with glasses on is unmarked.

Right: The dog with the lorgnette has a paper label that reads "Relco Japan".

$20-25 each

Three dog figurines with glasses, the one in the middle is unmarked, the other two are both stamped "7555".
$20-25 each

Decor D'Arf

(The Band Plays On . . .)

Poodle playing cymbals, unmarked.
$10-15

Two black poodles – one on the left is playing drums, the one on the right is playing a horn, both are unmarked.
$10-15 each

Three Poodles playing instruments, a french horn, a clarinet, and a cello, unmarked.
$10-15 each

The Poodles playing instruments,
a violin, a horn, and a drum, unmarked.
$10-15 each

Two Angel Poodles playing
instruments, on the left he is playing
a violin, on the right a harp,
the harpist is stamped "1317".
$20-25 each

Three Poodle Musicians, each are unmarked,
the percussionist in the center is stamped "Patt. 3807".
$10-15 each

This Music Box unites two popular 50's motifs, poodles and ballerinas.
$40-45

Madame Poodle tries on wigs as she sits atop her music box. (I was told by a dealer that these music boxes were used in jewelry stores to display rings).
$50-60

Madame and Monsieur Poodle with pups, both sets are by Lefton and came in three different colors pink, blue or white.
$10-15 per set

Mother with pups, stamped Kreiss & Company.
$15-20

Tiny Poodle set w/paper label that reads "Bradley Bone China Japan".
$5-10 per set

This angora trimmed family of poodles was popular in the late 1960's.
$8-12

Black Poodle, 10" tall, spaghetti design, the pups are missing.
$45-55
$75-100 with Pups

Poodle Mother, her puppies and chain are missing.
$15-20 with Pups

Three matching poodles in different positions, with gold collars, unmarked.
$15-20 a set

Mother with pups chained to her, she has a paper hat that makes cleaning difficult.
$10-15 a set

Left: Mother with pups on leash, unmarked.
$10-15 a set

Right: Mother giving pups a bath.
$15-20

Three matching poodles, unmarked.
$10-15 a set

Two different sets of Mothers with their pups, both are unmarked.
$10-15 per set

Decor D'Arf

(Italy)

Poodle holding ball,
marked "Made in Italy".
$15-20

Poodle figurine, 14" tall,
hand painted, marked "Italy".
$45-60

Left: Three headed poodle figurine,
marked "Italy".
$15-20

Right: Large poodle with collar,
marked "Italy".
$15-20

Left: Poodle Head Cup/Planter, marked "Italy".
$10-15

Right: Poodle figurine, marked "Italy".
$10-15

Two different poodle figurines,
both are marked "Italy".
$25-30 each

Decor D'Arf

(Jane Callender's)

Black poodle gentleman with white top hat, is a "Jane Callender Blue Ribbon Winner".
$50-60

Cowboy poodle with two smaller poodles, all three are "Jane Callender made in California".
Cowboy – $60-70
Smaller two – $30-40

Dutch clipped poodle, "Jane Callender".
$60-70

Decor D'Arf

(Parasol Pooches)

Two poodle figurines with parasols, unmarked.
$20-25 each

Gentleman smoking a pipe, unmarked.
$12-16

Lady with a parasol and purse, stamped "577B Patt." It is hard to find her complete with a parasol.
$20-25

Two poodles balancing parasols while riding unicycles.
$20-25 each

Madame with a parasol takes her pups for a stroll, no label.
$20-25 a set

Decor D'Arf

(Poodles on the Furniture)

Black Mother poodle and her pup on a loveseat, and in the matching chair a white poodle naps.
$15-20 each

Poodle Couple relaxes in matching chairs, one reads the newspaper, the other sips coffee, unmarked.
$20-25

Left: Poodle Lady with fan sits in a throne-like chair.

Right: Poodle with red cap stands on chair.

$15-20 each

Decor D'Arf

(Costumed Canines)

Two Cowboy Poodles, with guns, unmarked.
$15-20 each

French Cowboy Poodles, both marked "Japan".
$15-20 each

Three Poodle Firemen, all are stamped "Patt. 5262" with a paper label that reads "Made in Japan".
$20-25 each

Poodle Fireman at a hydrant with a hose, unmarked.
$15-20

Bathroom novelty.
$20-25

Poodle with a scooter from
Niagara Falls Canada.
$15-20

Black Poodle on Skis with a
green cap, marked "Japan".
$15-20

Pink Poodle with blue rhinestone eyes,
smoking and wearing a fancy hat.
(Smoking was politically correct in the 1950's).
$20-25

Periwinkle is unmarked,
rare color and matte finish.
$20-25

Three poodles with slaw or rug cut fur,
two smaller ones have rhinestone eyes.
$15-20 each

Poodle Bride with spaghetti design, has a choice of many potential grooms that wore top hats, canes and bow ties.
$15-20

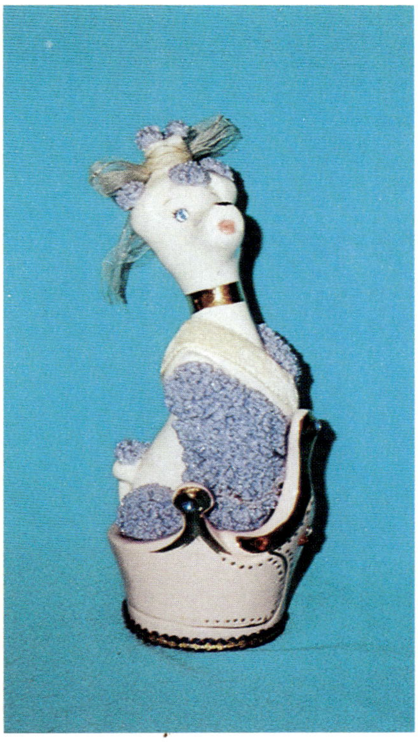

This queen of the poodles most likely had a king long ago.
$15-20

Madame is coifurred in the latest from Paris.
$15-20

A pair of poodles dressed
for a night on the town.
$10-15 a pair

This pink lady is coifurred with red felt hat. She has long black lashes framing blue rhinestone eyes, unmarked.
$8-12

Vaudevillian pair with hats and canes.
The left one has a paper label that reads "Relco Japan",
the one on the right is unmarked.
$12-16 each

Poodle with hat, spaghetti design,
unmarked.
$8-12

Poodle with hat and large tie,
unmarked.
$15-20

Sitting poodle with rhinestones
on its body and eyes, paper label reads
"Thames Hand Painted Japan".
$15-20

Two pink French poodles in Christmas attire.
The one on the left is unmarked, the one
on the right is stamped "1GX2255".
$20-25 each

Black poodle with a basket, hat,
and pearls, unmarked.
$10-15

The black poodle on the right delivers the "Times" to the black poodle by the mailbox. The one with the newspaper is marked "Lefton", the other is unmarked.
$15-20 each

Three different French poodles with berets.
$12-16 each

A Male and Female Poodle talking on the telephone. He is stamped "Kreiss & Co."
$35-40 a pair

Decor D'Arf

(Off the Wall Poodles)

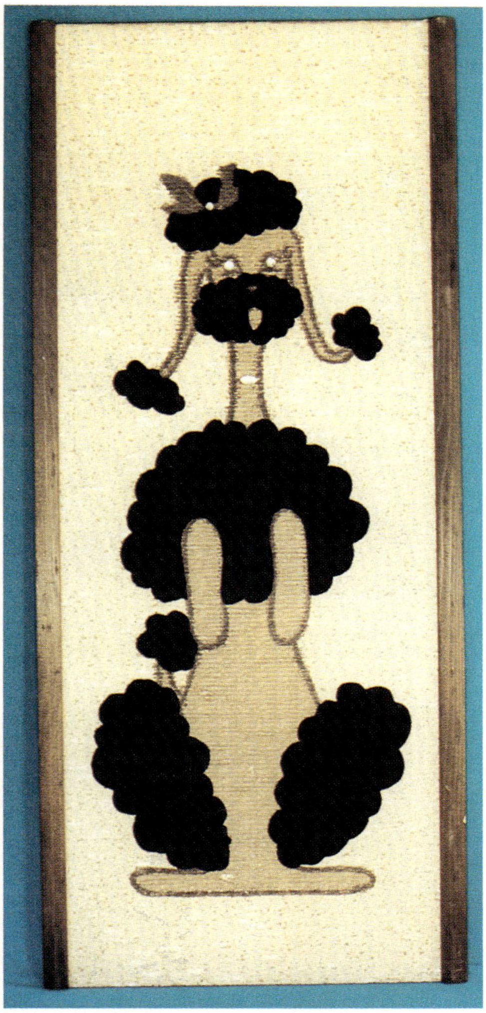

Unfinished Wall Hanging, stamped "Joy Art Co. California".
$15-20

Glittering poodle on a diamond shaped canvas. This was probably made from a kit.
$15-20

Mosaic Wall Hanging, probably made by an amateur craft person from a kit.
$12-16

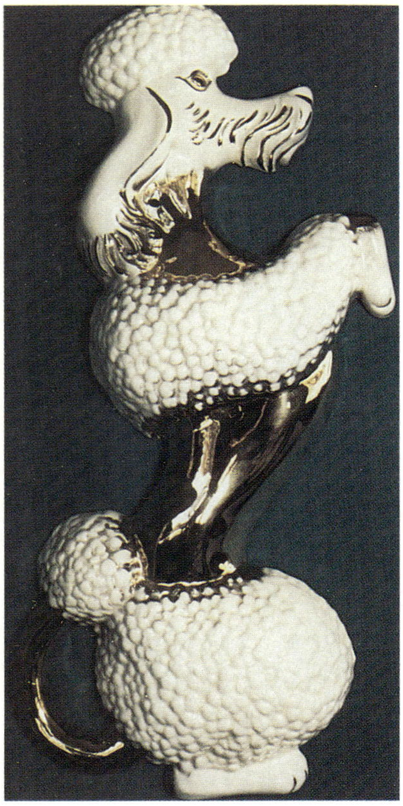

These gorgeous wall plaques are huge (9" x 21") and were made in at least two color variations, unmarked.
$100-125 pair

Picture called "A Friendly Game of Blackjack", many 50's poodles seem to have gambling problems.
$15-20

Picture of a poker game with a poodle waitress carrying drinks to the canine players.
$20-25

Three piece wall plaque set, part of the in mold mark is illegible, the mark ends with "of Calif.".
$25-30 a set

Plaster poodle plaques,
unmarked.
$15-20

Plaster plaques made at the tail
end of the poodle craze,
by "Miller Studios 1969".
$10-15 a pair

A whimsical print in a plastic
frame, by Margery d'Arty.
$10-12

1950's Wallpaper, shows various
party animals, hard to find,
by "Joliet Mills".
$25-40 per roll

Wallhanging, labelled.
$40-50

A print of a poodle admiring itself in a mirror, great detail was implemented by Margery d'Arty.
$15-20

Another popular French theme, the sidewalk cafe is the background for this print by "George Buckett 63".
$18-22

Doe-eyed brood in the foreground of the ever popular 50's theme "Champ de Mars" and of course poodles. Signed "George Buckett 63".
$18-22

Pair of ceramic plaques with a paper label that reads "Hand painted by Helen DeTar California".
$40-50

Pink poodle plaques, "Hand painted by Helen DeTar California".
$40-50 a pair

Wire trimmed trivets signed "Yentom", also has a paper label that reads "A California Decorative Original by Jaru".
$40-45 a pair

CHAPTER 4

Doggie Duds

Straw purse with lucite handle, marked "Princess Charming by Atlas Hollywood Fla.".
$25-30

Studded poodle on purse, marked "Jolles Original".
$30-35

Plastic purse with poodles on it, marked "JR Florida USA".
$35-40

Woven purse with two poodles pictured on it, marked "Princess Charming by Atlas Hollywood Fla."
$20-25

Child's purse
$6-9

Sequined dog on wool purse, "Graceline Master Purse".
$45-50

Cotton purse with poodles playing ball, it was stamped for embroidery.
$8-10

White woven purse, with two black poodles, labeled "Princess Charming By Atlas Hollywood Fla.".
$20-25

Velvet poodle purse, circa 1940's.
$35-40

Wooden purse signed "Gary Gails Dallas".
$15-20

Wooden purse with two poodles pictured, handle is missing, marked "Handcrafted by K-Wes Pebble Beach Texas".
$20-25 with handle

Cosmetic bag, no label.
$10-15

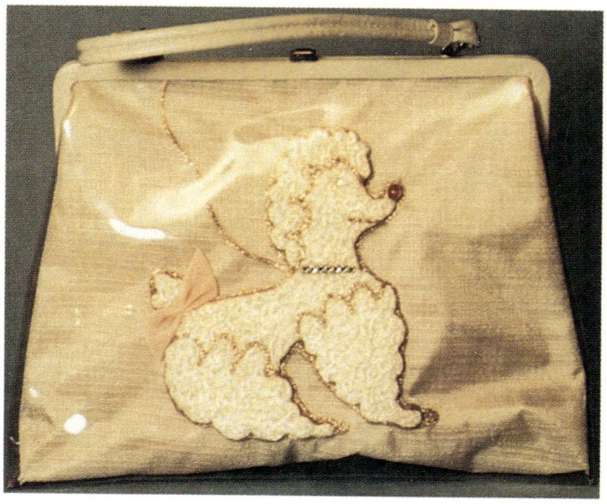

Plastic poodle purse, no label.
$30-35

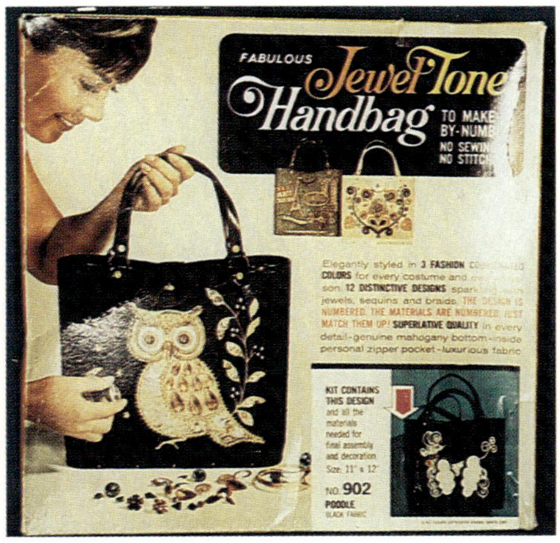

This Jewel Tone black purse with glittering Madame, strolling through the Camp de Mars. Purse and kit shown here, the kit is by-number.
$35-50

Handkerchief – **$4-6**

Yellow purse has a goldtone angelic winged poodle clasp, marked "Korea made of genuine patent leather".
$30-35

Brightly colored scarf with multi breeds – **$7-10**

Hanky with pom pom – **$5-7**

Wicker poodle purse that has a leash for a handle, and the head opens the purse. Marked "Maybelle Marie Birch California".
$40-50

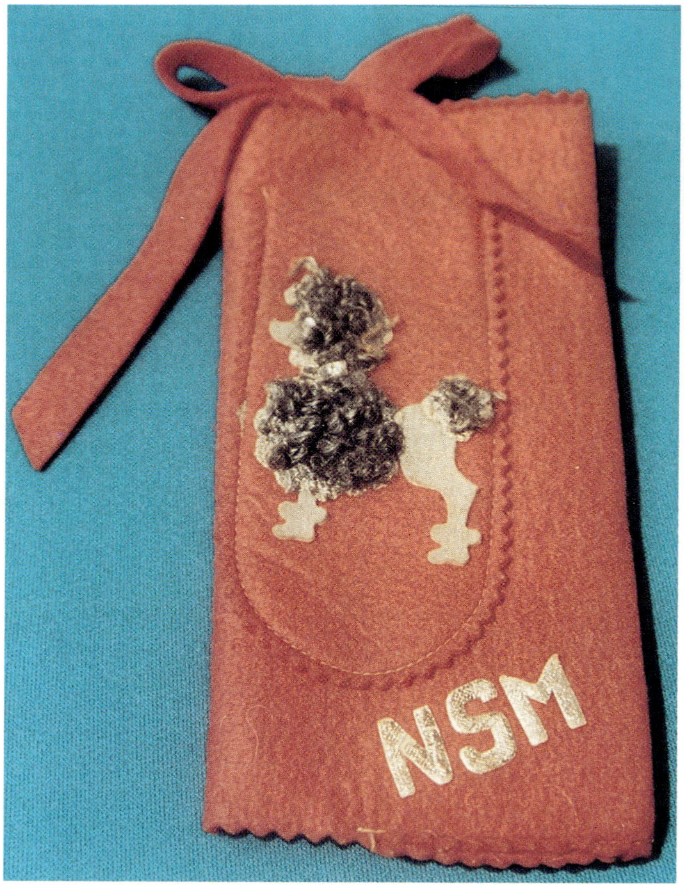

Eyeglass holder with a poodle on it.
$4-6

Child's sweater with beaded poodles, labeled "Ultra Lon Dorset Knitwear 100% Orlon".
$30-40

Cotton hanky with poodle admiring herself in a hand mirror.
$3-5

The clown on this skirt has his poodle jumping through hoops. The skirt appears to be home made from one of the preprinted kits.
$25-30

A 1950's Poodle Skirt, labeled "Len Nay Originals a division of Len Jay Originals".
$60-75

Silk scarf with poodles on it, not labeled.
$4-6

A brown embroidered poodle on a handkerchief with scalloped edges.
$3-4

Silk scarf, no label.
$8-10

Rhinestone earrings.
$40-60

Three poodle pins, all have different colored rhinestone eyes, unmarked.
$8-12 each

Poodle pins with red rhinestone eyes, unmarked.
$6-8 each

Poodle pins, unmarked.
$6-8 each

Poodle pins & charm, unmarked.
$6-8 each

Poodle pins, unmarked.
$4-6 each

Poodle pins, unmarked.
$8-12 each

Gold poodle pins, unmarked.
$8-10 each

Poodle pendant, unmarked.
$10-15

Poodle pins, unmarked.
$6-8 each

Poodle pins with blue rhinestone eyes, unmarked.
$10-15 each

Poodle head brooch,
faux topaz with goldtone trim.
$14-18

Poodle brooches, bakelite.
$35-45 each

Two different sizes of poodles, unmarked.
$20-25 a set

Left: Poodle with red rhinestone eyes, unmarked.

Right: Poodle with pearl eyes, earrings, and necklace, unmarked.
$8-12 each

Left: Poodle is attached to a lamp post by a rhinestone chain.

Right: White poodle with rhinestone eyes and a pearl on its back, unmarked.
$12-16 each

Poodle pins, they come in several colors, marked Gerry.
$20-25

Left: Blue poodle, the head is on a spring, rhinestone eyes, unmarked.
$10-12

Right: Poodle with rhinestone eye, the head also turns, marked "Napier".
$30-35

Beaded pooch brooch sticks out her tongue.
$15-20

Poodle with rhinestones, unmarked.
$6-8

Poodle pin, unmarked.
$6-8

Stylized hammered metal brooch, unmarked.
$10-12

Left: Poodle by "Sara Coventry".
Right: Christmas Poodle by "Gerry".
$8-12 each

Red poodle pin, unmarked.
$4-6

Wiry poodle, unmarked.
$8-10

Sterling silver poodle, unmarked.
$25-30

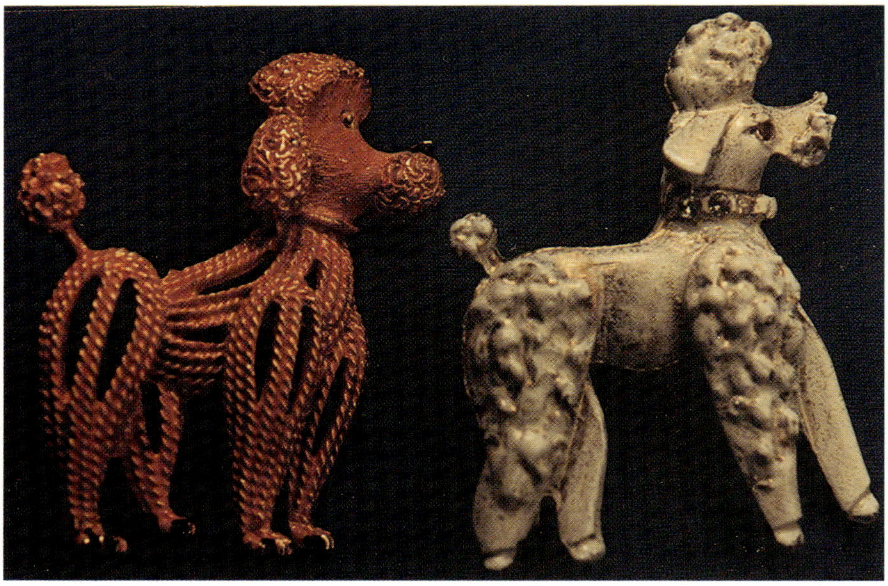

A Red and a white poodle pin, both are unmarked.
$4-6 each

Napkin Ring with red
rhinestone eyes, unmarked.
$8-10

Black rhinestone brooch, unmarked.
$30-40

Lady and two cowboy poodles.
$18-22

Copper Pendant, unmarked.
$10-15

Pair of poodles with red eyes and collars, unmarked.
$15-20 a pair

Left: Poodle pin with rhinestone eyes, unmarked.

Right: US pin with poodle hanging from chain, unmarked.
$10-12 each

Girl walking her poodle, unmarked.
$12-16

Left: Large poodle with red collar, unmarked.

Middle: Gentleman with hat and cane, unmarked.

Right: Poodle with rhinestone eyes and green tie, unmarked.
$8-10 each

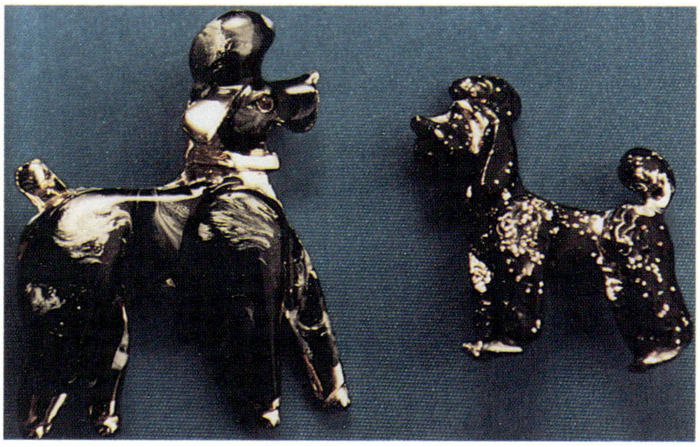

Two different silver poodle pins, unmarked.
$4-6 each

Charm Bracelet with lots of poodle charms, unmarked.
$30-35

Large goldtone poodle, unmarked.
$6-8

Lacy pom poms poodle,
decorates this goldtone pendant.
$10-15

Prancing poodle with rhinestones, unmarked.
$12-16

Poodle with big pearl breast, unmarked.
$12-14

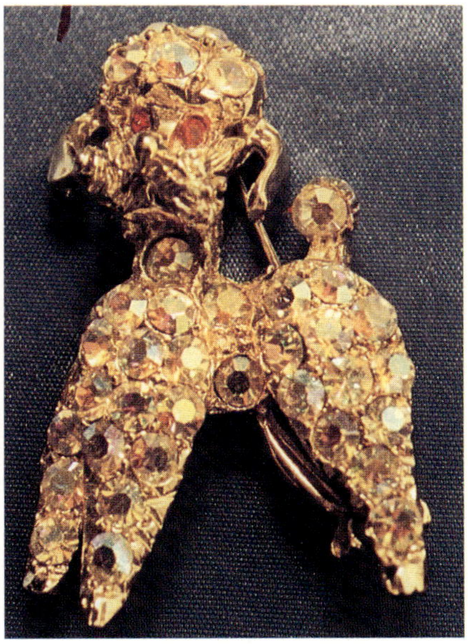

Head to toe rhinestones embellish the goldtone poodle brooch, umarked.
$15-25

Two antique finished poodles with red rhinestone eyes, unmarked.
$8-10 each

Copper poodle pin with a large bow on her head and a green rhinestone eye.
$15-20

Left: Poodle with a big pom pom on head and red rhinestone eyes, unmarked.

Middle: Tall poodle with rhinestones all over the neck and back, unmarked.

Right: Begging poodle, marked "S. Coventry".

$15-20 each

Two rhinestone covered poodles, unmarked.
$12-16 each

Two very similar pins,
Left: Poodle marked "Gerry",
Right: Poodle marked "Sarah Coventry".
$15-20 each

Two poodles apparently from the same mold, unmarked.
$6-8

Unmarked poodles.
$12-14

Delicate stylized brooch with goldtone and blue enamel highlights, unmarked.
$16-18

Rhinestone poodle marked BSK.
$12-14

Two goldtone brooches, notice the paisley trim on the one at the right.
Both are unmarked.
$12-16

Two Poodle pins, one with Christmas sock hat, both are marked Gerry.
$15-25 each

Left: Rhinestone poodle, unmarked.

Right: Black poodle pin with turning head and is marked Napier.

$25-35 each

Left: Sledding poodle with rhinestone eye, by "Corel".

Right: Stocking stuffer poodle by "Gerry".

$18-22 each

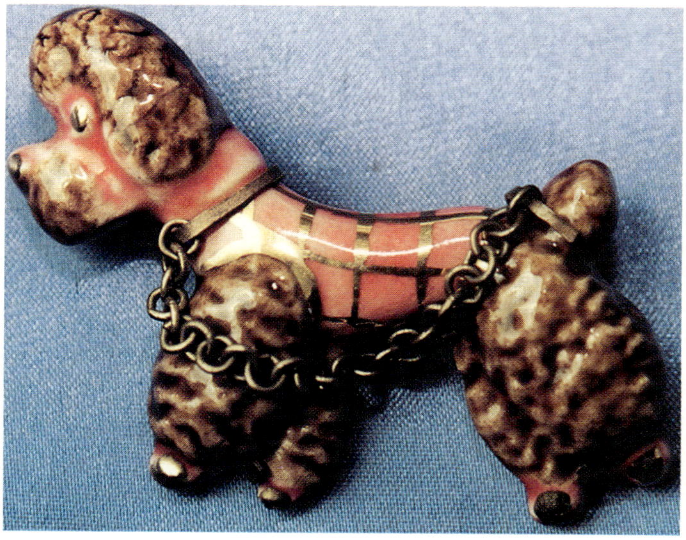

1950's Brooch enamelled with chain.
$20-25 each

Two poodle pins with rhinestone eyes, both are unmarked.
$10-12

Left: Googly eyed poodle with bow tie, unmarked.
$8-10

Right: Poodle with a big rhinestone in its belly, unmarked.
$18-22

Sterling silver pin that resembles a lion.
$25-35

Assorted goldtone charms, unmarked.
$8-10 each

Lacy pendant with blue rhinestone eyes, unmarked.
$10-15

All three poodle pins unmarked.
$6-8 each

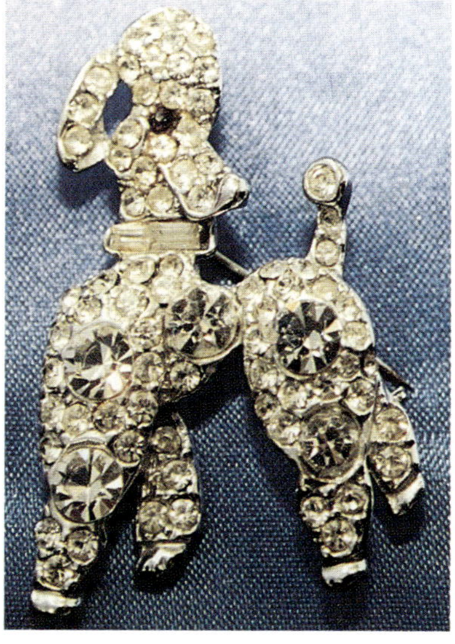

Rhinestone poodle pin, unmarked.
$12-16

Two rhinestone poodles, unmarked.
$20-25 each

Two poodle pins, unmarked.
$5-7 each

Two poodles with green rhinestone eyes, unmarked.
$12-14

Two silver poodle pins, unmarked.
$10-12 each

Two stylized poodles, unmarked.
$7-10 each

Left: This pin is marked and number Boucher.
(I've heard from several dealers that it's a limited edition).
$50-60

Right: This pin is one of many imitations
from the original Boucher.
$15-20

This pin marked "Gerrys" came in
many color variations and
with and without rhinestones.
$8-10

Left: Rhinestone & baquette
poodle is marked PEL.
$18-22

Right: Black poodle is marked
"Mamselle".
$10-12

Two Copper poodles, the one on the left is unmarked, the one on the right is marked Monet.
$14-18 each

Two goldtone poodles with rhinestones, unmarked.
$10-15 each

Left: Another Boucher copy cat pin.

Middle: This poodle is marked "Avon".

Right: This goldtone poodle with green rhinestone eyes is marked "SA".

$14-18 each

Left: A 1940's unusual diapered pup, unmarked.
$10-12

Right: Poodle with a green rhinestone eye, unmarked.
$6-8

Left: Pearl and rhinestone poodle, unmarked.

Middle: Goldtone poodle with rhinestone eyes.

Right: Angora covered goldtone poodle.

$6-8 each

Two goldtone poodles, both are unmarked.
$10-12 each

Compact with tassle, unmarked.
$25-30

A three piece purse set includes
cigarette holder, compact and comb.
$45-60 a set

Glittered compact with paper label that reads
"Marhill Genuine Mother of Pearl".
$35-40

Left and Center: Compacts, unmarked.

Right: Cigarette holder and velvet bag, unmarked.

$25-40 each

Compacts, lipstick holder, and comb
all with poodle motif.
$25-40 each

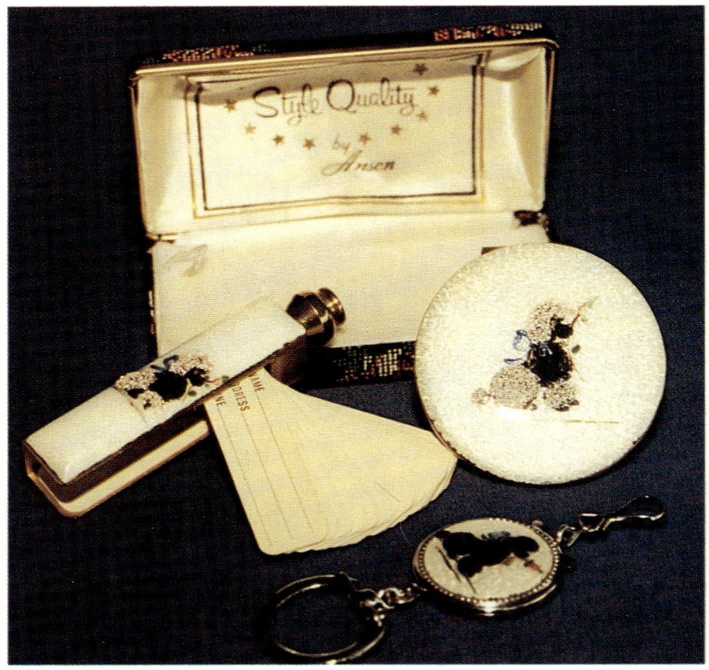

Three piece set by "Anson", includes
an address holder, compact and key chain.
$45-60 a set

Two compacts, both are unmarked.
(Usually unmarked because they originally had a paper label
or they came in a box).
$25-30

Poodle with glitter ornamentation on unmarked
compact with pink velvet bag.
$35-40

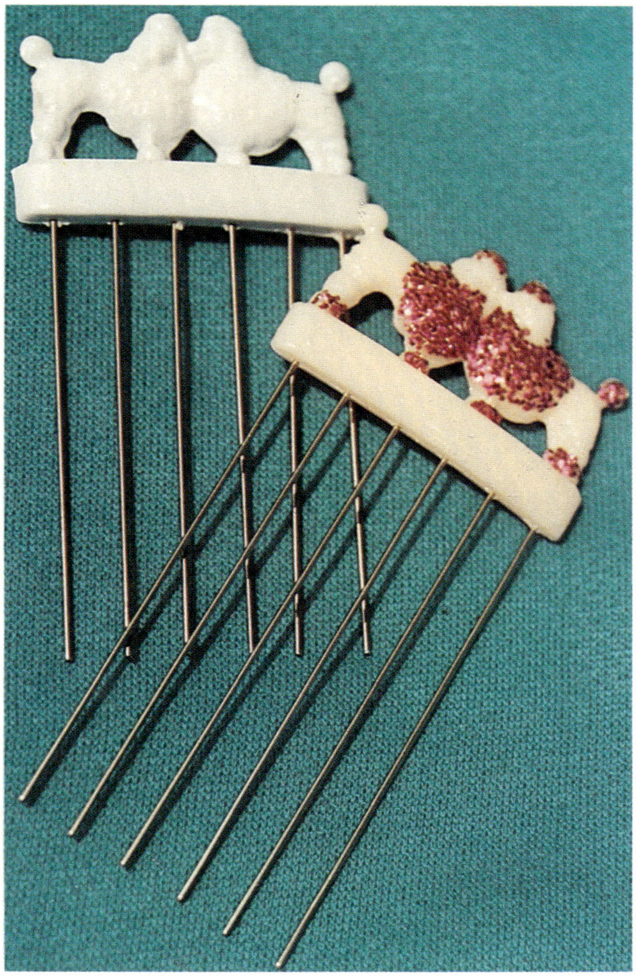

These two hair lifts appear to be the same. The one with the pink glitter is marked "Glamour Lift by Kurtell & Co." The other one is unmarked.
$4-6 each

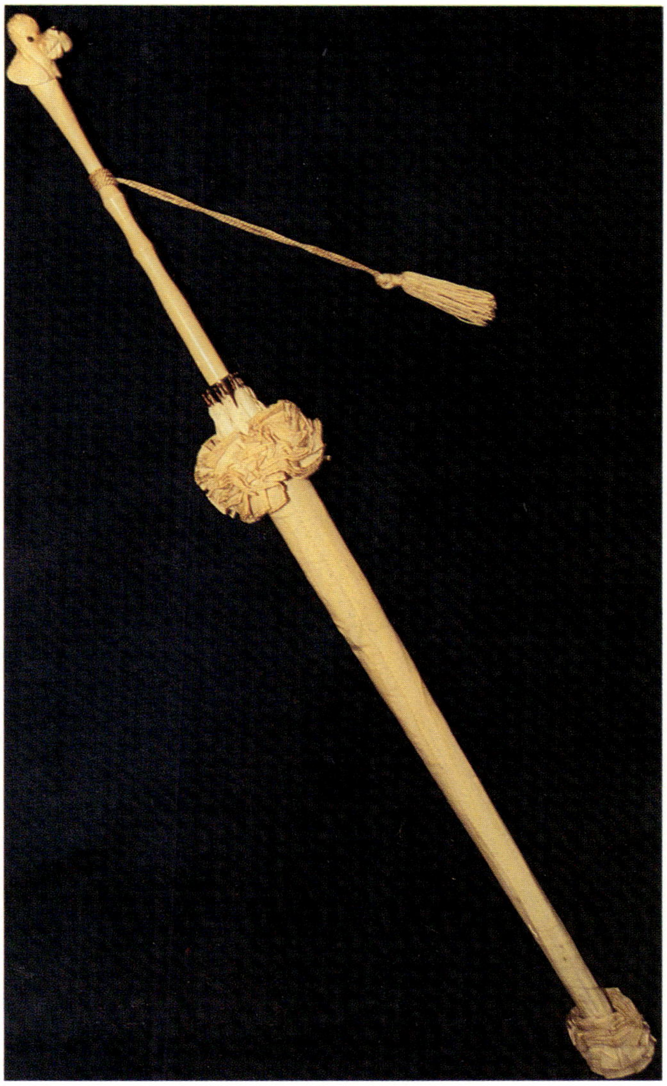

Parasol with poodle handle.
$10-15

Goldtone purse-size Saccharin Holder with tiny tongs.
$18-22

CHAPTER 5

Sew Many Poodles

Pincushion with removable top, enameled, marked "Florenza".
$30-35

Enameled pincushion is also a nodder, marked "Florenza".
$30-35

Pincushion/thimble holder/ tape measure, marked "Florenza".
$30-40

Pincushion, unmarked.
$10-15

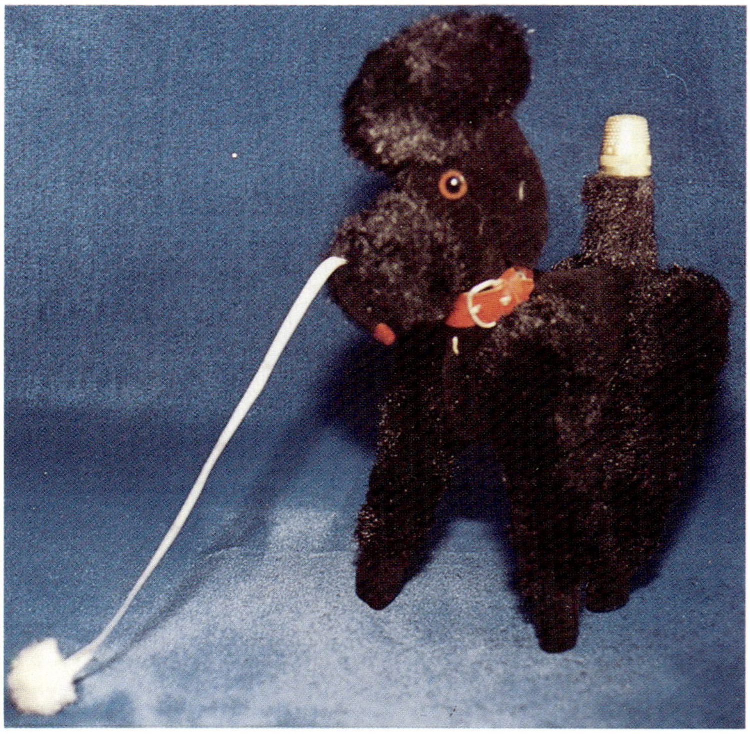

Plush sawdust filled pet, serves three different purposes, marked "Japan". – **$20-25**

Left: A scissor holder and pincushion.

Right: A pincushion and tape measure.

$15-20 each

Wicker Sewing Basket with thread tray insert, no label.
$15-20

Three Towels, pre-stamped for embroidery, no label.
$3-6 each

Simplicity was one of several companies offering poodle patterns.
$1-2

Childs poodle skirt pattern 1956. Poodle skirts were found in catalogs as early as 1953 and as late as 1959.
$2-4

White cotton fabric with red stylized poodles.
$10-15 per yard

Ceramic poodle buttons. **$3-4 each**

CHAPTER 6

Poodles on Paper

Poodlettes stationary by Whiting.
$10-12

Rare store display items.
$30-40 a pair

This Halloween-Autumn decoration may have been part of a store display.
$15-20

Metal enameled saucer.
$8-12

Advertising piece for Lanvin My Sin perfume.
$40-60

Poodle Decals.
$4-6

Poodle Swizzle Sticks.
$1-2 each

Poodle Gift Wrap
$2-6 per roll or package

Greeting Card
$2-6 each

Delicate canines embellish a birthday giftwrap set.
$4-6

Canine bedecked playing cards.
$1-2 per card

Greeting Card
$2-6 each

Poodle writing tablet.
$5-7

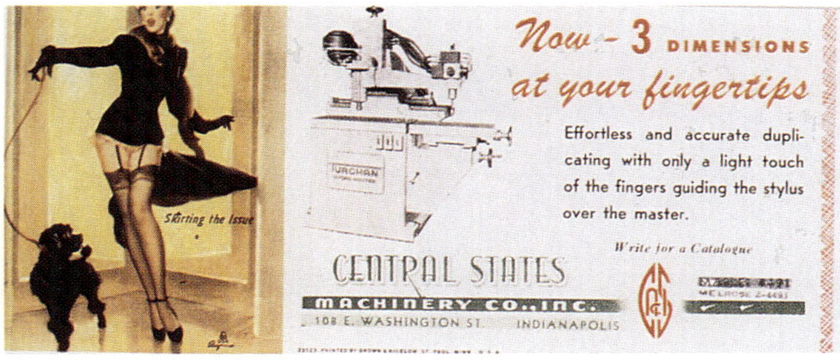

Central States Machinery Co., Inc. ad.
$4-6

The poodle craze was just beginning in 1946. This cover model Stephanie Allen holds her favorite pet and wears a "poodle cloth coat". The clothes are by Maximilan Furs. The dog is Surrey Parfume by Dogs Inc. and the Coat-a-crome by Tony Venti.
$3-6

"Pantaloon", Little Golden Book
$10-15

"Puppy Playhouse" features six pullout dogs including Curly the poodle. Copyright 1951, by Polygraphic Co. of America, no author.
$10-12

Playtime Poodles by Helen Wing, no copyright date listed.
$6-8

Page 28 of "Puppy Playhouse".

Crepe Paper Party Placemate
$1-2

Giftwrap.
$2-6 per sheet or package

Giftwrap.
$2-6 per sheet or package

Postcards.
$1-2 each

Coaster.
$1

Paper Napkins and Coasters.
$.50-1 each

"Striking" poodles adorn many matchbooks.
$1-3 each

Greeting Cards – **$2-6 each**

Greeting Cards – **$2-6 each**

All are Greeting Cards shown on this page – **$2-6 each**

All are Greeting Cards
shown on this page – **$2-6 each**

Matinee Poodle Centerpiece – **$10-15**

Collier's Cover with Doris Day and French Poodles in color to match all different outfits – **$2-8**

Jantzen Sunclothes ad – **$2-8**

Old Gold Cigarette ad – **$2-8**

Calvert Reserve ad – **$2-8**

Old Gold ad – **$2-8**

Pepsi Cola ad – **$2-8**

1956 Oldsmobile Ninety-Eight ad – **$2-8**

KAL KAN
BURGER ROUNDS
KAL KAN
CHICKEN
KAL KAN
TUNA
KAL KAN
BEEF LIVER
KAL KAN
M.P.S. CHUNK
KAL KAN
KIDNEY
KAL KAN
STEW
KAL KAN
KAL KAN
HORSE MEAT
N – THE PREMIUM PET FOOD LOS ANGELES, CALIFORNIA
Diamonds are a pet's best friend
R1

Kal Kan ad – **$2-8**

CHAPTER 7

Dogs in Toyland

Pink lady poodle made from a combination of vinyl, cashmere and lame, unmarked.
$20-25

Left: "Dream Pet"

Right: "Holiday Fair Medaya & Co.", N.Y.C. made in Japan.

$8-12 each

Vinyl dog made in Japan.
$4-6

Court Jester Poodle, marked "Japan".
$8-12

"Mimi" was produced by C & M Srery Co., Hollywood Calif., "Cutie Pets", made in Japan.
$10-15

Mother carrying her pup in a basket, unmarked.
$15-20

Black and white poodle, unmarked.
$10-15

"Madame Alexander" poodle.
$35-45

White chenille lady, unmarked.
$6-8

Green beaded toy sports rabbit fur pom poms.
$6-8

Two stuffed toys from the fifties.
$4-8 each

"Snobby" is one of many poodles made by Steiff.
$30-35

"Tammy Dream Pet by R. Dakin & Co.", #1018 came in at least three colors: black, white, and pink. Her legs are jointed.
$10-15

Right: Mom and pup "Dream Pets".
Left: Unmarked Poodles (possibly the Dad?)
$10-15 each

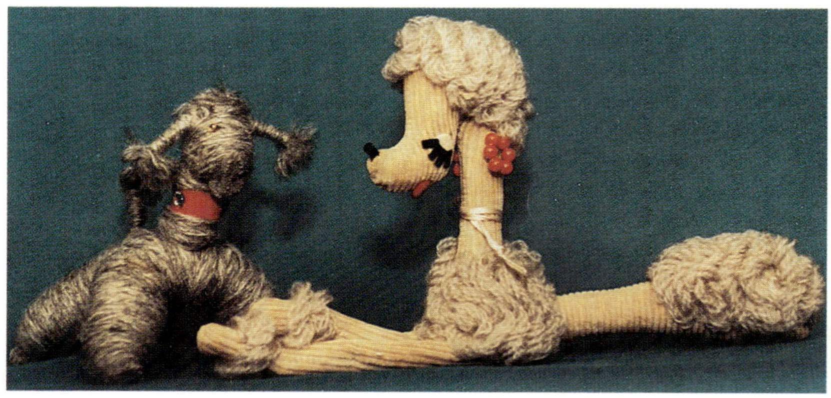

Unmarked poodles.
$6-8

Tan faux leather and cashmere "Dream Pet".
$8-10

Two more color variations of the Dakin "Dream Pet" series.
$8-12 each

Pink doll bed (not assembled), and the side rails to the bed.
$18-25

Children's tin dishes by "Ohio Art", are coveted by collectors in several different fields.
$18-24 a set

Small tin tray signed "Melissa", (possibly a tip tray or snack tray).
$4-6

A doll poodle skirt.
$3-5

All four of these are "Breyers".
$30-40

Hard plastic toys, the one on the right has a magnet that attracts the metal in the ball.
$10-20 each

Child's metal trunk for doll clothes.
$18-22

Unmarked plush puppet with vinyl head.
$6-8

"Pelham puppet, made in England" was featured in F.A.O. Schwartz 1968 Christmas Catalog for $5.95.
$80-100

Dogs in Toyland
(I Make A Motion)

Pull toy poodle marked "Empire".
$15-25

Penny the Poodle by Marx Toys in 1963, came in a reverse color combination. Her actions include: standing, sitting, turning her head and barking.
$25-35

Poodle push puppet, unmarked, and new.
$3-5

Mechanical battery operated toy from the 1960's, marked "Japan".
$30-35

Musical canine artist plays a lullaby and goodnight arm moves with brush by "Common Wealth Toys and Novelty Fifth Ave. NY".
$35-50

Two unusual pink wind-up poodle toys from the 1950's, both marked "Japan".
$40-60

Plush musical toy with original box and tag by Ideal.
$40-60

Cragston Sleepy Musical Poodle, with five different mechanical movements.
$35-50

Dogs in Toyland

(Squeeze Me)

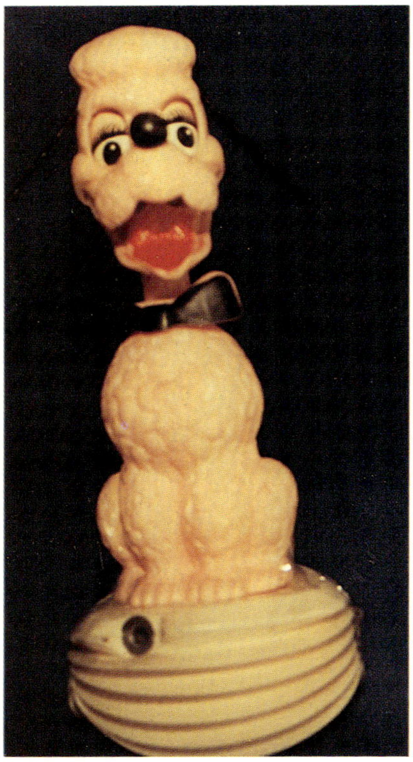

Squeeze the accordion base and his ears fly out and his mouth opens.
$12-16

Assorted rubber squeeze toys.
$10-20 each

"Sun Rubber Co. 1963".
$8-12

Two rubber squeeze toys that appear to be singing a duet.
$10-15

Peteena T.M.

TV's newest collector doll sensation!

A new concept in dolls . . . a Paris inspired fashion poodle that will sell like the Paris originals!

Every now and then a fantastic new item comes along. Imaginative! Daring! Almost shocking! Yet you know it will be a sensation. Peteena is that kind of item! She's a sophisticated creation that is in step with the times . . . in tune with today's active younger generation. They will take to her because she is what she is . . . unusual, different, provocative! And television will introduce and sell Peteena to the millions of youngsters waiting to buy her. Get enough of her today . . . because she'll be the hottest thing in the toy business tomorrow!

#9005 PETEENA FIGURE

Peteena is a doll of a poodle and a poodle of a doll! She's 9½" tall and a real go-go girl who is bendable in every direction. She has genuine rooted hair, a furry tail, and real eyelashes. And she comes boxed in a teenie-weenie bikini outfit with top, bottom, hat, sun glasses and bracelet that are right in step with the times. 1 DOZ. . . 9 LBS.
$4.00 SUG. RETAIL

#9010 PETEENA SCHOOL-TIME OUTFIT

Snappy French motif sweater, stretch pants, skirt, shoes, shoulder bag, books with strap, and flag. Just like little French school girls. 11" x 11" x 1". 1 DOZ. . . 8 LBS.
$4.00 SUG. RETAIL

#9011 PETEENA SLICKER OUTFIT

When it rains in Paris, little girls bundle up. Peteena is no exception with her rain coat, rain hat, boots and umbrella too. Every piece is Paris inspired. Display package 11" x 11" x 1". 1 DOZ . . . 8LBS.
$3.00 SUG. RETAIL

#9012 PETEENA SKI OUTFIT

Peteena's turtle-neck sweater, ski pants, ski parka, boots, fur hat, goggles, are straight from the latest ski slope fashion at St. Moritz. Also, one pair of ski poles, one pair of skis, one pair of mittens. 11" x 11" x 1". 1 DOZ. . . 10LBS.
$5.00 SUG. RETAIL

#9014 PETEENA FORMAL OUTFIT

Little girls will be thrilled when they dress-up their Peteena in her formal evening wear for L'Opera. Included in this package, an evening gown, silk stockings, long evening gloves, evening purse, fur piece, bracelet, one pair earrings, one brooch. 11" x 11" x 1". 1 DOZ . . . 8 LBS.
$4.00 SUG. RETAIL

#9015 PETEENA BALLERINA'S OUTFIT

With this great Peteena outfit, little girls will turn pirouettes. Set comes with top and bottom leotards, ballet dress, floral head piece, one pair of ballet slippers. Styled after the National French Ballet. 11" x 11" x 1". 1 DOZ. . . 8 LBS.
$5.00 SUG. RETAIL

#9018 PETEENA ASSORTED BOXED GOODS

2 each of following items: #9010, #9011, #9014
3 each of following items: #9012, #9015. 1 DOZ. . . 10 LBS.
SUG. RETAIL $52.00 PER ASST.

#9020 ASSORTMENT

One Doz. of 9005, Peteena Figure. One Assortment of 9018 Peteena Boxed Items. 2 Cartons, Wt. 19 Lbs.
SUG. RETAIL $100.00 PER ASST.

peteena
by Hasbro

peteena
The Pampered Poodle
Ooh La La

peteena
Zero Cool
Fashions for the Lively One

peteena
Twinkle Toes

"Peteena The Pampered Poodle" by Hasbro 1966. Came with 6 outfits including the one she is wearing.
$45-60

"Zero Cool" one of Peteenas outfits. According to a Hasbro spokesperson, Peteena had a one year run.
$18-25

CHAPTER 8

Miscellaneous

(This Chapter is in no particular order, these items were received after the book was already in process).

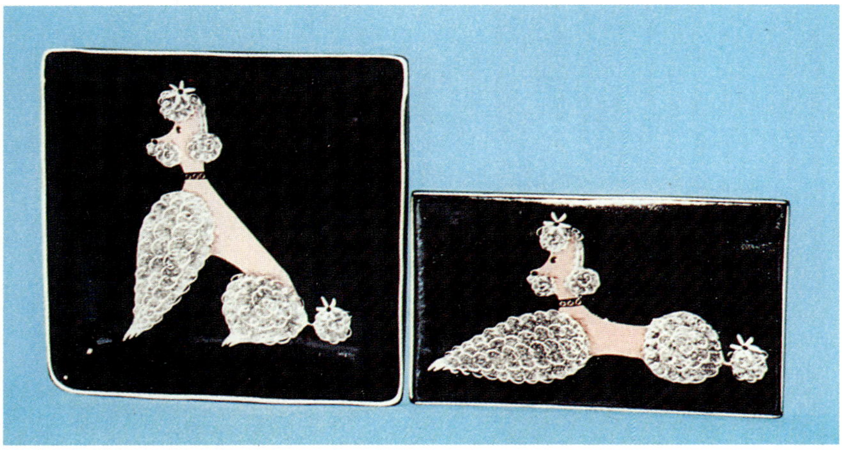

"Hedi Schoop" – **$40-45 ea.**

"Kay Finch" figurine.
$50-60

This figurine was made by California Artist "Hedi Schoop".
$75-90

Plaque marked "Ceramicraft San Clemente Calif."
$20-25

High quality unmarked bookends.
$25-35 a pair

Toilet Brush Holder
$15-20

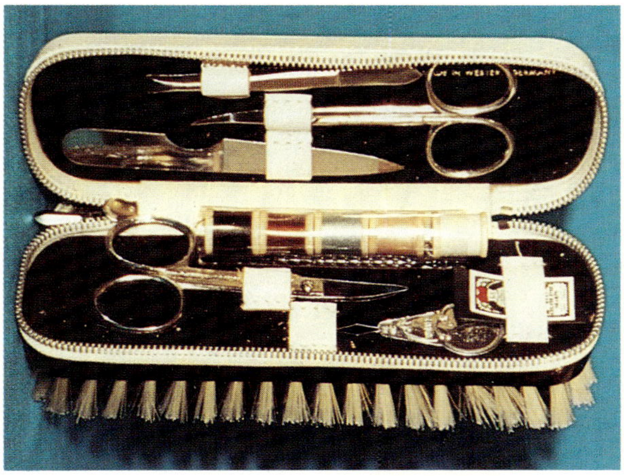

Lint Brush with manicure and sewing kit.
$10-15

Barber Pole, (also shown in the cover photo) originated in the 1970's and is still in production through William Marvey Co. St. Paul, MN.
$450-500

This shower curtain arrived at the last minute and was photographed wrinkles and all.
$15-20

"Fiffy" battery operated toy, Japan.
$40-50

Bath Mat
$15-20